# Becoming
# Your
# True Self

## Daniel C. Jordan

Baha'i
Publishing
Trust

Becoming Your True Self
by Daniel C. Jordan

Revised edition
© 1993 The Bahá'í Publishing Trust
27 Rutland Gate
London SW7 1PD


Designed and typeset by The Art House


Illustrations © Hugh Sean O'Rourke


British Library Cataloguing-in-Publication Data

A catalogue record for this book
is available from the British Library

ISBN 1-870989-27-9

# CONTENTS

# INTRODUCTION

*Becoming Your True Self* offers a concise and challenging analysis of human nature, and reveals how each of us can achieve both fulfilment and happiness in our lives. It explores the search for truth and meaning in a secular world, and presents the worldwide Bahá'í community as a successful model of personal and social transformation. Musician and educator Dan Jordan explains how the followers of the nineteenth century Persian prophet Bahá'u'lláh are inspired to realise their true potential, and to contribute to the healing and development of the wider community in which they live.

First published in 1968, this remarkable and influential essay demonstrates how the personal struggle for transformation of millions of Bahá'ís across the globe is being reinforced by the radical social processes within the Bahá'í community. It shares a vision of an ever-advancing civilisation where the rights of all people are protected and our collective potential more fully realised.

O Lord! Should the breath of the Holy Spirit confirm the weakest of creatures, he would attain all to which he aspireth and would possess anything he desireth. Indeed, Thou hast assisted Thy servants in the past and, though they were the weakest of Thy creatures, the most insignificant of those who lived upon the earth, through Thy sanction and potency they took precedence over the most glorious of Thy people and the most noble of mankind. Whereas formerly they were as moths, they became as royal falcons, and whereas before they were as brooks, they became as seas, through Thy bestowal and Thy mercy. They became, through Thy most great favour, stars shining on the horizon of guidance, birds singing in the rose-gardens of immortality, lions roaring in the forests of knowledge and wisdom, and whales swimming in the oceans of life.

'Abdu'l-Bahá

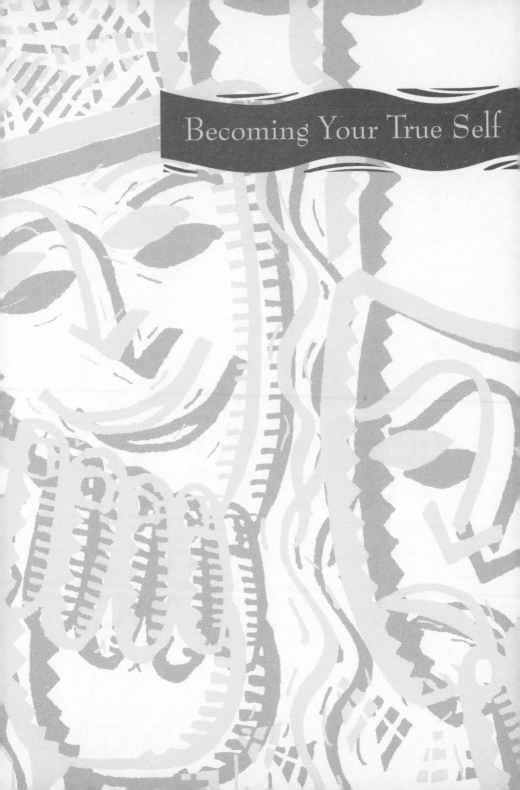

# Becoming Your True Self

OVER A HUNDRED YEARS AGO, Bahá'u'lláh, the Founder of the Bahá'í Faith, made the staggering claim that His Revelation would be the chief instrument by which the unification of the human race would take place, and through which world order and world peace would ultimately be established.

Few will disagree that if we are to progress from the present state of world turmoil and conflict to world peace and unity, social institutions and the human beings making them up will have to undergo a radical transformation. Therefore, whoever is truly interested in world peace must also be interested in how such transformation can be brought about. It is on this crucial issue that the Bahá'í Faith attracts those who seek a practical model for positive social and personal change. In just over 100 years the Bahá'í Faith has grown to become the second-most geographically widespread of the independent world religions.[1] Embracing people from more than 2100 ethnic, racial and tribal groups, it is quite likely the most diverse organised body of people on our planet. Its unity challenges prevailing theories about human nature and the prospects for our common future. Throughout the world there is an increasing interest in

*If we are to progress from the present state of world turmoil and conflict to world peace and unity, social institutions and the human beings making them up will have to undergo a radical transformation.*

the process of transformation fostered by the teachings of
Bahá'u'lláh. This book is one attempt to explain how
these revolutionary teachings enable us to discover and
become our true selves.

It would be wise to confess that it is not possible to
discover or understand all the forces latent within
Bahá'u'lláh's vast revelation which nurture and direct the
process of transformation. But the Bahá'í Writings shed a
great deal of light on the way in which the Bahá'í
Faith transforms the lives of its adherents by
releasing their human potential.

*Millions everywhere are longing to become fully noble, rather than remain imprisoned and abased by a false sense of their own nature.*

Interest in how human potential can be released is
personal and practical rather than academic, for millions
everywhere are longing to become, as Bahá'u'lláh
expresses it, fully noble, rather than remain imprisoned
and abased by a false sense of their own nature.

Of course Bahá'u'lláh's teachings concerning the
transformation process are stimulating to the mind.
However, knowledge of them has also a practical purpose,
for conscious knowledge of what is happening during that
process helps to consolidate the gains and enables one to
identify and accept, often through painful experiences that
may at first appear needless and cruel, opportunities
for further growth.

Personal transformation is a fundamental reason why people are attracted to the Bahá'í Faith, develop conviction as to its truth, and finally become Bahá'ís. The reason is simple. People who come in contact with the Bahá'í Faith, and feel themselves being transformed by it, have an experience that is self-validating. No one can take that experience away from them, and no intellectual argument can make it appear insignificant or unreal. To feel oneself becoming the best of what one can potentially be constitutes the highest joy. It promotes a sense of self-worth, obviates the need for expressing hostility, and guarantees a compassionate social conscience — all prerequisites of world unity and peace.

*Personal transformation is a fundamental reason why people are attracted to the Bahá'í Faith, develop conviction as to its truth, and finally become Bahá'ís.*

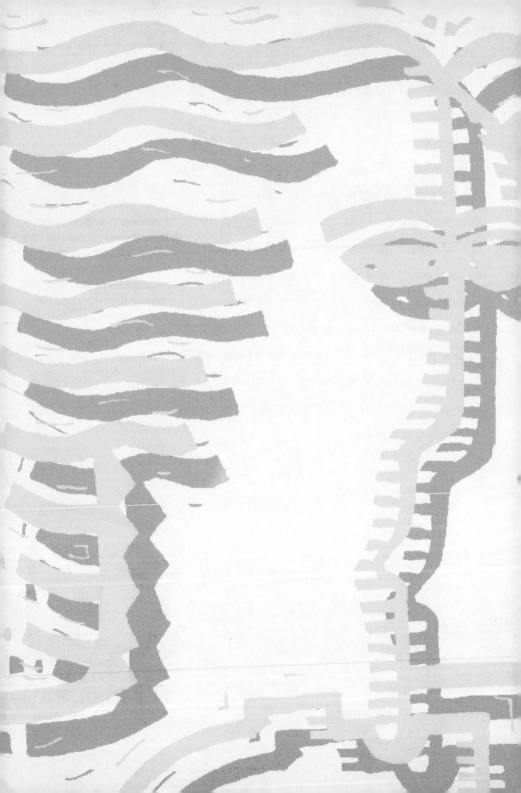

# The Nature of Human Potential

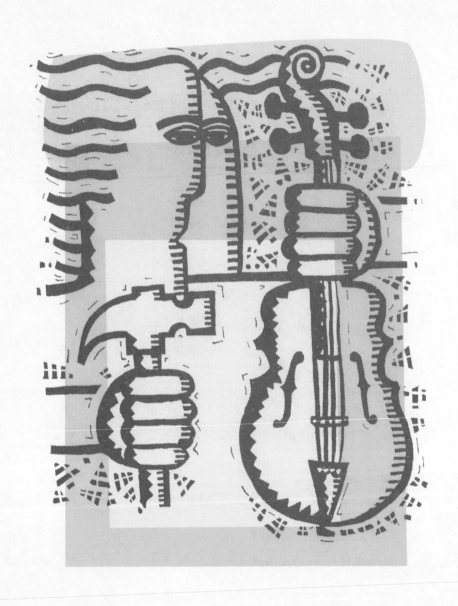

BUT WHAT IS THE 'BEST' of what one can potentially be? Bahá'u'lláh teaches that the highest expression of the self is servitude. The degree to which this highest station of servitude can be achieved depends on the degree to which our basic human powers or capacities can be released. The process of becoming one's true self, then, is synonymous with that process of developing basic capacities, and dedicating them to the service of humanity. The daily decisions and actions which reflect this 'becoming' are essentially religious in nature, for Bahá'u'lláh equates work of all kinds performed in a spirit of service — in the spirit of that highest human station — with worship. Those who begin to see the religious nature of 'becoming' will not only recognise a profound new dimension in work and worship, but will also see religion in a new light. They will begin to understand that when the force which continually enables one to grow disappears from any religion, it is time for it to be renewed, for religion devoid of that force is little more than empty rituals, meaningless dogmas, and social conventions which block the expression of the human spirit and impede social progress.

*Those who begin to see the religious nature of 'becoming' will not only recognise a profound new dimension in work and worship, but will also see religion in a new light.*

Service to humanity is given quality by the depth and character of the capacities of the person rendering it.

What are these capacities? Bahá'u'lláh identifies them as the animating purpose behind our creation: to know and to love God. Here the two basic powers or capacities of knowing and loving are clearly specified and linked to our purpose — our reason for being. Thus, for a Bahá'í, becoming your true self means the development of your knowing and loving capacities in service to humankind.

This understanding gives substance to the notion of spirituality. A spiritual person is one who knows and loves God, and who is committed to the struggle of developing these knowing and loving capacities for service to humanity. By definition, then, being closed-minded about something, refusing to look at new evidence — blocking the knowing capacity, or reacting to others in unloving ways — are all signs of spiritual immaturity or spiritual sickness.

*Becoming your true self means the development of your knowing and loving capacities in service to humankind.*

All other virtues can be understood as expressions of different combinations of these basic capacities of loving and knowing as they are applied in different situations. The loving capacity includes not only the ability to love, but also the ability to be loved — to attract love. We cannot have lovers without loved ones. If we do not know how to be loved or cannot accept it, then we frustrate

others who are struggling to develop their capacity to love.
When someone does not accept love, the person offering
it normally experiences this as rejection, which does
untold amounts of damage, particularly in young children.

The knowing capacity also includes a knowledge of
how to learn and how to teach. Teaching and learning
are reciprocal aspects of the knowing capacity. No teacher
is a good teacher who cannot learn from his or her pupils,
and no good pupil fails to question the teacher, so that
both teacher and pupil learn.

*In order to know, we must love learning; if we are to love, we must know how to love and how to be loved.*

Each capacity supports and facilitates the development
of the other. In order to know, for instance, we must love
learning; if we are to love, we must know how to love and
how to be loved.

These two capacities constitute the basic nature of
human potential. From a Bahá'í point of view, true
education refers to a drawing out or development of
potential to the fullest extent possible. Unfortunately,
much of contemporary education is concerned only with
the presentation of information rather than drawing out
potential. For this reason, schools are primarily a place
where facts and ideas are dispensed by the teachers and
stored by the pupils. Consequently, diplomas and degrees

do no more than certify that certain kinds and amounts of information were dispensed, and that the recipient of the diploma was able to demonstrate at various points during the course of formal education that the information had been stored long enough to be retrieved and written down in an examination. Such degrees or diplomas say nothing about the loving or feeling capacity of the student, and therefore say very little about character — a word which refers to a person's ability to apply knowledge constructively and to express love for humanity.

*True education should be concerned with the character of the whole person, rather than just a small part.*

Furthermore, it has been demonstrated that if the loving capacity is blocked in any way, there will be learning problems and the development of the knowing capacity will be impaired. That is why a school system based on the narrow 'dispensing-of-information' view of education can never adequately serve the needs of society. True education should foster development towards the achievement of the highest station — servitude — and must therefore be concerned with the character of the whole person, rather than just a small part.

# Faith and the Release of Human Potential

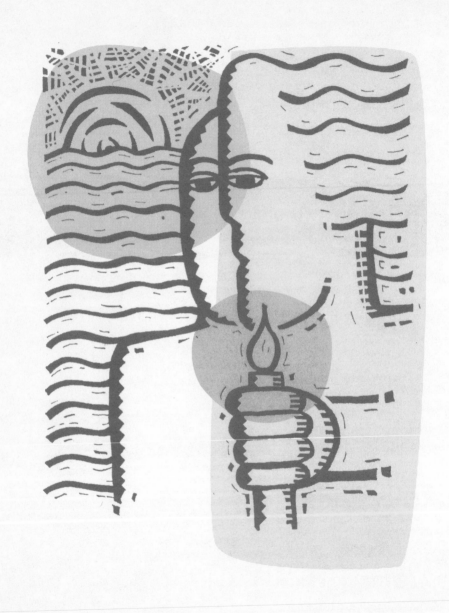

IT IS ONE THING TO DESCRIBE the nature of human potential, and another to release it. The Bahá'í Faith does both.

The basic source of the power for transformation is the Writings of Bahá'u'lláh. Exposure to His Writings nurtures the development of faith — the first prerequisite for transformation. Basically, faith refers to an attitude towards the unknown or unknowable which ultimately enables one to approach it in a way that something more of it becomes known. It thus represents a special interplay of the two basic capacities of knowing and loving. In essence, faith means a loving of the unknown or unknowable — an attraction to whatever is unknown and a capacity to approach it. Since, as Bahá'u'lláh affirms, God is unknowable, it takes faith to become attracted and related to God.

*We all have a kind of cosmic hunger, a need to be related to all things, including the infinitude of the universe.*

We all have a kind of cosmic hunger, a need to be related to all things, including the infinitude of the universe. This is a natural by-product of consciousness. Since we experience ourselves as beings distinct from all other things in the universe, we feel compelled to find out how we stand in relationship to every other thing, and this includes how we are related to those unknown or unknowable things which also exist in the universe.

The ultimate unknowable mystery of the universe is called by many names: Allah, Jehovah, God, Supreme Being. Because we have the capacity for faith — a particular attitude toward the unknown — humankind has, throughout history, responded to the Founders of the world's great religions who came to manifest the attributes of that unknowable mystery in the universe — God — and satisfy our cosmic hunger. Thus, faith is one important expression of our purpose, which is to know and to love God.

*Faith is one important expression of our purpose, which is to know and to love God.*

If our basic capacities are knowing and loving, and if we are created in the image of God, then knowing and loving must be among the attributes of God. Bahá'u'lláh indicates that this is so when He says, 'O Son of Man! Veiled in My immemorial being and in the ancient eternity of My essence, I knew My love for thee; therefore I created thee, have engraved on thee Mine image and revealed to thee My beauty.'[2]

Further, if God is unknowable and if we are created in the image of God, then we may expect something in ourselves also to be unknown. This unknown is the as yet unexpressed potential within us — latent capacities for loving and knowing. In a very dramatic way, Bahá'u'lláh points to that vast unknown in ourselves when He quotes the verse of a well-known Persian poet: 'Dost thou reckon thyself only a puny form/When within thee the universe is folded?'[3] In another verse, Bahá'u'lláh says, 'Ye are My treasury, for in you I have treasured the pearls of My mysteries and the gems of My knowledge.'[4]

None of us knows our own capacity for love, or how much we can learn. Just as we had to have faith before we could learn about the attributes of God, so must we have faith before we can know something of ourselves. We must love — be attracted to, have a particular attitude towards — that unknown in ourselves if it is to be released. If we relate satisfactorily to the unknown in ourselves, we will be able to relate to the unknown in others. In other words, we have to accept others not only for what they presently are, but also for what they can become; otherwise, we impede their process of transformation and keep them from becoming their own true selves.

> *We have to accept others not only for what they presently are, but also for what they can become; otherwise, we impede their process of transformation and keep them from becoming their own true selves.*

This is why people who have given up on themselves, who have stopped becoming, and have therefore betrayed their own potential, will find all their relationships with other human beings disturbed, unsatisfying, and even painful. To accept and relate to other human beings just as they are at a particular moment in time precludes the development of anything more than superficial relationships. To achieve deeply meaningful relationships with other human beings, we have also to accept the unknown possibilities within them, for that acceptance constitutes one important source of their courage to become. In more personal terms, if you do not accept the unknown possibilities in yourself, you will not be able to establish anything more than superficial relationships with other human beings, and you will not be able to help them develop their potential — or develop your own.

*If you do not accept the unknown possibilities in yourself, you will not be able to establish anything more than superficial relationships with others, and will not be able to help them develop their potential — or develop your own.*

Since one's potential is an extremely important part of one's reality — in fact, the basis of future growth — it must be accepted by others and play a part in human relationships before one can feel totally accepted. Total acceptance on the part of others constitutes a special kind of trust that is very difficult to betray. It is one very important source of benevolent pressure to become, and one of the most significant criteria of real love and friendship. This kind of pressure reciprocated between two human beings will spiritualise any relationship, but has

particular significance for marriage. It forms the spiritual
basis of Bahá'í marriage.

The necessity for reciprocity in this kind of relationship is
clearly expressed by Bahá'u'lláh in The Hidden Words,
where He states, 'O Son of Being! Love Me that I may
love thee. If thou lovest Me not, My love can in
no wise reach thee. Know this, O servant.'[5.]
In this verse, God commands, through His
Manifestation, that we love Him and accept Him
in spite of the fact that He is unknowable. Being
attracted to the unknowable is the essence of faith. If there
is no faith, no attraction to that primary mystery — God,
then we become alienated from the mystery in our own
selves and cut off from the power to grow and develop. The
statement quoted above starts with 'O Son of Being' and
ends with 'know this, O servant.' Thus, in that very short
verse, the two basic capacities of loving and knowing are
again emphasised in the contexts of being and serving.
It connects the process of being or becoming with
that highest station of servitude.

> *Being attracted to the unknowable is the essence of faith. If there is no faith, no attraction to that primary mystery – God, then we become alienated from the mystery in our own selves and cut off from the power to grow and develop.*

# Anxiety and the Unknown

FACING ANY UNKNOWN IS NOT EASY. The prospect of it, particularly when facing the unknown in ourselves, is always accompanied by anxiety. An external unknown is nearly always perceived as a potential threat to our security, for it brings up a question that represents an intrinsic unknown — do we, or do we not have what takes to deal successfully with that external unknown?

*The only successful way to deal with anxiety is to treat that energy as a gift and find a concrete goal for it which will serve the more basic goal or purpose of developing capacities for loving and knowing*

Anxiety has all the qualities of a fear reaction, except that it usually has no clear-cut object. Both fear reactions and anxiety reactions are characterised by a rapid energising of the system which prepares it to deal with an emergency situation. One can handle the fear reaction more easily, since the threatening object is identifiable and be removed or avoided. In the case of anxiety, the system goes into a state of preparedness for an emergency when it is not clear what the emergency is. Without any object, it is difficult to know what action to take, and the system is never quite certain when to declare the emergency over. Anxiety may thus be seen as energy without a goal.

The only successful way to deal with anxiety is to treat that energy as a gift and find a concrete goal for it which will serve the more basic goal or purpose of developing capacities for loving and knowing. Determining what that goal should be in specific terms is perhaps the most universally creative human act. It entails assuming a risk and stepping into the unknown, bearing the burden of doubt, yet always hopeful of discovering some new capacity or some new limitation (which is also part of one's reality). Being attracted to that unknown in ourselves is faith; being able to utilise the energy from anxiety by formulating a goal and taking steps toward it is courage. Thus faith, doubt, anxiety and courage are all basic aspects of the process of transformation — the release of potential. If there were no unknowns, there would be no doubt or anxiety; and with no doubt or anxiety there would be no need for faith and courage.

*Faith, doubt, anxiety and courage are all basic aspects of the process of transformation — the release of potential.*

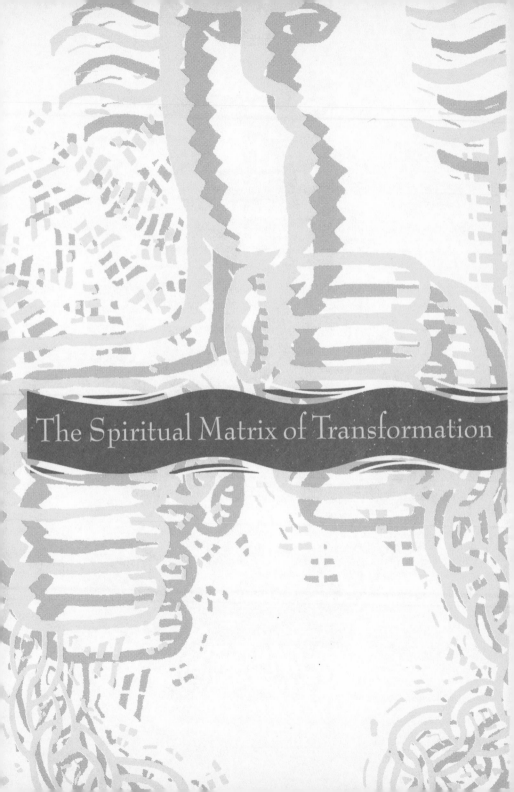

The Spiritual Matrix of Transformation

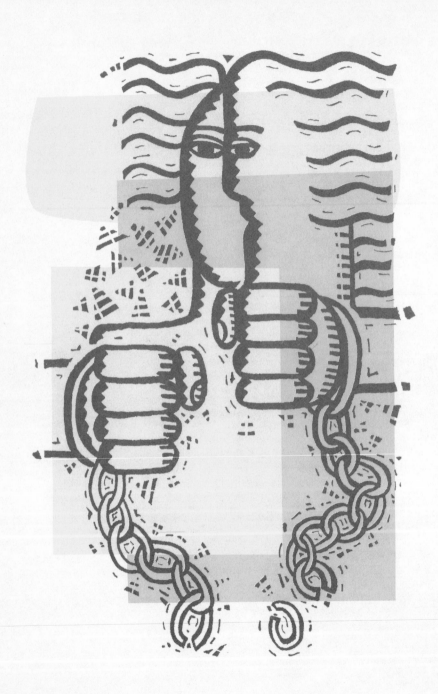

THE POWER OF THE BAHÁ'Í FAITH to transform human beings by releasing their potential stems directly from the fact that it keeps doubt and anxiety from reaching unmanageable proportions, and provides an incentive and motivation to deal with them constructively through faith and courage. Bahá'u'lláh indicated that the primary source of the power for transformation comes from an acceptance of His Word — the Word of God. His Writings are often referred to as 'the creative word' precisely because people have felt themselves being created anew as they become more and more exposed to it. Bahá'u'lláh clearly affirms that if you want to become transformed, you must 'immerse yourselves' in the 'ocean' of His words.[6]

Immersion in that ocean begins the process of transformation by creating an awareness of the essential nature and purpose behind our creation. When we read Bahá'u'lláh's words, our loving and knowing capacities are awakened and developed. As we continually explore His Writings, we begin to see ourselves differently, and to see our environment differently. As we begin to see ourselves and our world differently, we begin to feel differently about things. As we begin to feel differently, we begin to behave differently. Behaving differently is the tangible manifestation of having embarked upon the adventure of becoming your true self.

*As we continually explore Bahá'u'lláh's Writings, we begin to see ourselves differently, and to see our environment differently.*

The Writings of Bahá'u'lláh, therefore, serve as that intervening force which enables us to become free from all those attachments and fears which keep us imprisoned and unable to take that risky but creative step into the unknown. We know that human beings are often changed by intense experiences of one kind or another. Immersion in the ocean of Bahá'u'lláh's words is not just reading; it is an experience for the whole person, which can become intense enough to free one from ties to the status quo and to set us forth on the purpose of our destiny. As we are freed from crippling attachments to what other people think of us, we are less likely to be manipulated by them — imprisoned by them — and develop instead a source of intrinsic motivation.

*Immersion in the ocean of Bahá'u'lláh's words is not just reading, it is an experience for the whole person.*

The Writings of Bahá'u'lláh also reduce general anxiety and doubt to manageable proportions by making sense out of human history and the world's present state of perpetual crisis. This means that we need not pretend the crises do not exist, or refuse to face them. Thus understanding something of the problems which face us not only reduces anxiety but attracts courage.

A further source of courage stems from Bahá'u'lláh's indication, in general terms, of the kinds of goals which are legitimate and in keeping with the purpose of our creation. This gives us some guidance in taking that creative step of defining a goal which can be achieved by utilising energy from anxiety. We have an option here. We can either take that creative step of defining a goal and facilitate the transformation process, or we can refuse to do that, in any conscious way, and hope that the anxiety will finally go away by itself. Obviously, persons who have a great deal of guidance in what kind of goals to establish will be more apt to make conscious decisions in regard to defining goals. In the absence of such a definition, energy from anxiety is likely to be expressed in aggressive and hostile acts towards other human beings, whose reactions to the attack will very likely impede growth and development not only in themselves but in the persons to whom they are reacting. Thus, the Writings of Bahá'u'lláh stimulate our knowing and loving capacities in a unique way, by fostering faith and courage. This, in turn, serves to guarantee a continued growth and development of those two basic capacities. In other words, knowing and loving — when directed by faith and courage — will actually increase our capacity to know and to love. This is the release of human potential.

*The Writings of Bahá'u'lláh reduce general anxiety and doubt to manageable proportions by making sense out of human history and the world's present state of perpetual crisis.*

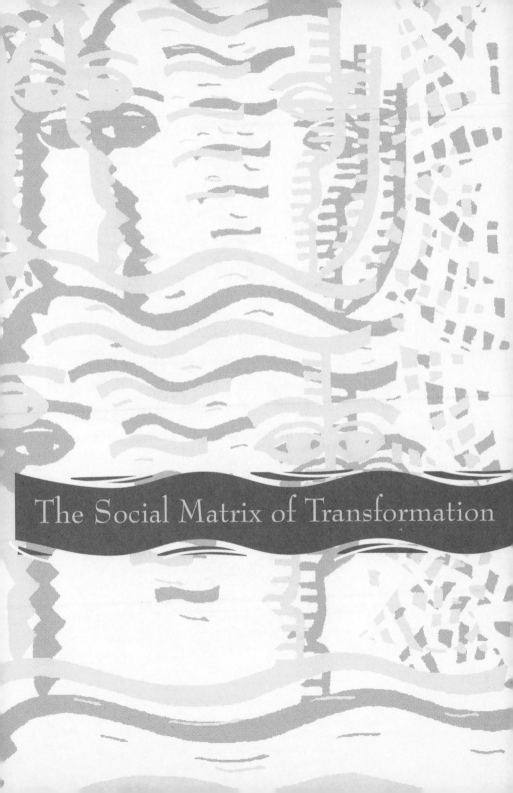

The Social Matrix of Transformation

BUT THIS IS NOT ALL OF THE PICTURE. Bahá'u'lláh has made provisions for the formation of communities whose institutions safeguard and promote the transformation of humanity. The Bahá'í community becomes, then, the social matrix of transformation.

Because of Bahá'u'lláh's affirmation of the principle of the oneness of the human race, Bahá'í communities are composed of people from diverse linguistic, racial, national, and religious backgrounds. This diversity in the Bahá'í community represents to every member many unknowns — or, in less euphemistic terms, the Bahá'í community is made up of people many of whom one would not ordinarily be attracted to or choose to be one's friends. It is well known that we tend to choose for our friends others who think the same as we do, who have similar tastes, and who like doing similar things. Within such a homogeneous group, one's transformation can easily come to a halt, for a set repertoire of responses is developed and there is no stimulus to develop new ones. That is why one of the most precious attributes of a Bahá'í community is its diversity.

*Bahá'u'lláh has made provisions for the formation of communities whose institutions safeguard and promote the transformation of humanity. The Bahá'í community becomes the social matrix of transformation.*

To join a Bahá'í community is to enter a family of extremely diverse people, with whom one will have to

BECOMING YOUR TRUE SELF

work and establish meaningful relationships. The first
thing one finds out is that the old repertoire of responses is
no longer adequate. So many different human beings
represent a great many unknowns, and trying to relate to
those unknowns creates energy (anxiety) which sets in
motion that reciprocal process of knowing and loving
through faith and courage. Defining a legitimate goal
which will constructively utilise the energy from that
anxiety will call forth a new repertoire of responses.
Each new response is a bit of one's latent capacity made
manifest — a release of human potential. Another way of
saying this is that the Bahá'í community offers more
opportunities for knowing and loving under growth-
fostering circumstances than can be found anywhere else.
Typically, a Bahá'í moves through a pattern of spiritual
evolution, starting with tolerance for the diversity of his or
her fellow community members. As knowledge is added,
that tolerance grows into understanding. When love is
added, understanding blossoms into appreciation. This
appreciation for diversity is the spiritual and social
opposite of ethnocentrism. The journey from
ethnocentrism, through the stages of toleration and
understanding, to a state of appreciation, always entails
many anxieties and doubts. We are often put in the

> *The Bahá'í community offers more opportunity for knowing and loving under growth-fostering circumstances than can be found anywhere else.*

position of not quite knowing what to do, or, if we do know what to do, we don't feel like doing it. These are tests which are pre-requisites to our transformation. 'Abdu'l-Bahá, Bahá'u'lláh's son, states unequivocally that without tests there is no spiritual development.

Here we come to a very critical issue. Tests can many times destroy an individual. 'Abdu'l-Bahá explains that if we turn away from God for the solution, the test may indeed destroy us. If we turn to God for the solution and if we have the loving support of other members in the Bahá'í community, we can pass the test successfully. Thus the Bahá'í community, because of its diversity, provides many of these tests which are essential to our spiritual development. At the same time, guidance from Bahá'í institutions and the commitment of the members of the Bahá'í community to accept each other for what they can become provides the courage to turn those tests into vehicles for spiritual development — for the release of human potential.

*Tests are pre-requisites to our transformation. Without tests there is no spiritual development.*

In brief, that is what Bahá'u'lláh means by 'adversity' when He states 'If adversity befall thee not in My path, how canst thou walk in the ways of them that are content with My pleasure'.[7] He encourages us not to be afraid of tests, but to welcome them as opportunities for spiritual

growth; ' My calamity is My providence, outwardly it is
fire and vengeance, but inwardly it is light and mercy.
Hasten thereunto that thou mayest become an eternal
light and an immortal spirit.'[8]

Thus, for a Bahá'í, happiness is not a life free from
anxiety or tension. That is the Bahá'í definition of
boredom. Happiness for a Bahá'í is having tests and
knowing how to summon the courage to pass them in such
a way that one's knowing and loving capacities are further
developed in service to humanity. Living in the Bahá'í
community provides the tests which become the
opportunities to acquire experience in translating abstract
principles into concrete realities. This gives faith a
foundation of conscious knowledge. It is this ever-
expanding conscious knowledge of how to apply
the Bahá'í principles in real situations that
consolidates the gains in spiritual development,
and provides the base for continued growth.

*For a Bahá'í,
happiness is not
a life free from anxiety
or tension. That is the Bahá
definition of boredom.
Happiness for a Bahá'í is
having tests and knowing ho
to summon the courage
to pass them.*

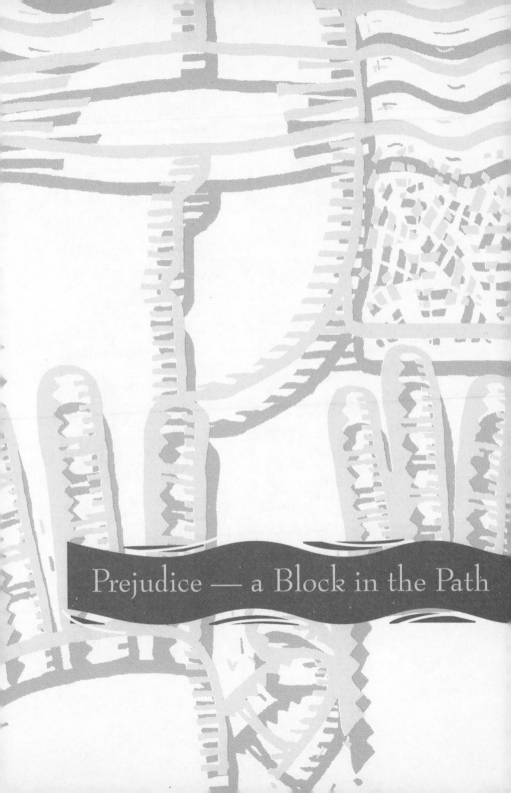

Prejudice — a Block in the Path

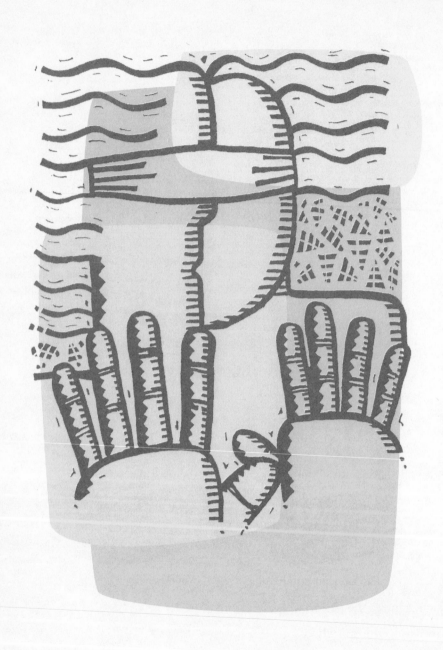

UNIFICATION OF ALL PEOPLES OF THE EARTH cannot take place if individual human beings are not united within themselves. Bahá'u'lláh indicated that He could find no human being who is inwardly and outwardly united. If one's knowing and loving capacities are in conflict, then one is not inwardly or outwardly united. The consequence is that one's words and deeds will not be in harmony.

The conflict of these capacities is reflected outwardly on another level. Science, for instance, may be regarded as an expression of humankind's knowing capacity and religion as an expression of the loving capacity. Bahá'u'lláh taught that science and religion must go hand in hand, or the conflict will cause destruction. Today we see how knowledge of nuclear energy without love creates a constant threat to our survival.

*A prejudice is an emotional attraction or commitment to falsehood or error.*

In a very basic sense, the word 'prejudice' refers to conflicts in the way these two capacities are expressed. A prejudice is a belief (a kind of knowing) in something that is not true coupled with an emotional confirmation (a kind of loving). In other words, a prejudice is an emotional attraction or commitment to falsehood or error. Actions based on that commitment are nearly always damaging to the person who is the victim of the action, as well as to the one who is carrying it out.

On a personal level, prejudice represents a definite blockage in the expression of human potential because the loving capacity has been used to impede the knowing capacity. In a fundamental sense, almost all neuroses and psychoses can be understood in terms of this kind of conflict. The goal of therapy, therefore, always has to be a removal of the blockage towards becoming one's true self by enabling the person's loving capacity to support his or her knowing powers, and vice versa.

*On a personal level, prejudice represents a definite blockage in the expression of human potential.*

On the social level, prejudice in action results in massive injustices ranging from discrimination and segregation to open violence and hostility organised in the form of wars. In like manner, this represents a definite blockage in the expression of society's potential.

Every barrier to the unification of the human race is sustained by prejudice — by widespread culturally determined emotional commitments to a falsehood. For this reason, Bahá'ís see the process of unification of humankind as being synonymous with the progressive eradication of prejudice. Before the barriers to unification can be torn down, the prejudices which support them must be abolished.

Why is prejudice so difficult to eradicate? One reason is that human beings often are unaware that they have a prejudice. Fundamentally, this is what bigotry is — being ignorant of one's ignorance while making bold and confident assertions of the rightness and truth of one's position. Bigoted persons are in a tragic position because they always avoid exposing themselves to any situation which would confront them with the fact that they have a prejudice. In concrete personal terms, how would you know that you had a prejudice against somebody who spoke another language or had a skin colour different from your own, if you never had the opportunity to be with such a person — if you never had an experience which would help reveal the error?

This is precisely why the Bahá'í community plays such an essential role in the progressive eradication of prejudice. It provides those very experiences which let its members know what their prejudices are. It is for this reason that the struggle for world unity takes place more inside the Bahá'í community than outside it. Outside the community, people can insulate themselves from those experiences which will reveal their prejudices to them, while continuing to have only those experiences which enable their perceptions to remain distorted and their commitment to falsehood strong.

*On the social level, prejudice in action results in massive injustices ranging from discrimination and segregation to open violence and hostility organised in the form of wars.*

For a Bahá'í, discovering a prejudice in oneself is always a test. The moment you recognise a prejudice in yourself, you know that you must struggle to eradicate it, not only because you know that being prejudiced will cause injustice to others, but also because your own spiritual development absolutely depends upon it.

What happens to a person with a blocked potential — a person who, for whatever reason, has not been able to find out how to become his or her true self? If the person is passive or introverted, he or she will tend to escape into a fantasy world, or withdraw into a world of drugs and alcohol, and will probably eventually become so dysfunctional that he or she may well have to be institutionalised. If the person is action-oriented and extroverted, he or she will be hostile and aggressive, and may eventually have to be institutionalised for committing crimes.

*The person who is in the process of becoming, whose loving and knowing capacities are being continually developed does not want to escape responsibility into a world of fantasy, nor does such a person want to fight, hurt, or kill.*

The point here is simple: the person who is in the process of becoming, whose loving and knowing capacities are being continually developed, does not want to escape responsibility into a world of fantasy, nor does such a person want to fight, hurt, or kill. It is impossible for human beings who feel their human potential being

released to engage in a war of any kind. Under such
circumstances there is absolutely no motivation for hostile
action. It is for this reason that Bahá'u'lláh claims that His
Faith and the Bahá'í community will be that agency
through which world peace will be ultimately established.

*It is impossible
for human beings who
feel their human potential
being released to engage in a
war of any kind. Under such
circumstances there is
absolutely no motivation
for hostile action.*

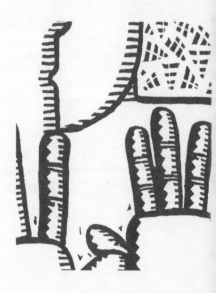

# The Kingdom of God on Earth

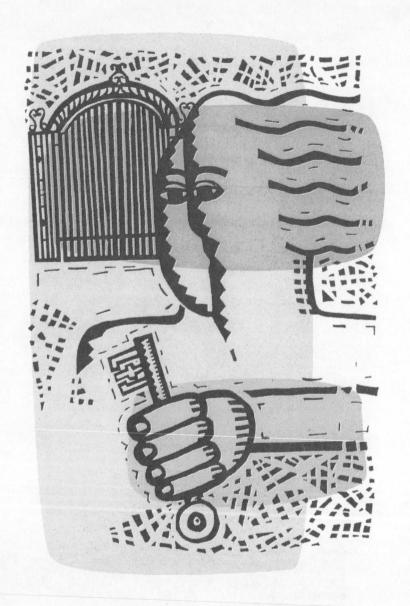

THAT UNKNOWN IN OURSELVES which the unexpressed potential represents has been referred to as the image of God. Becoming your true self means relating to that unknown in such a way that more and more of it becomes expressed. This always involves finding a goal for the energy from the anxiety that comes from facing that unknown.

*When the latent capacities for loving and knowing are organised and expressed on a social level we advance towards the establishment of the Kingdom of God on earth.*

This entire process has a social counterpart. What the image of God is to the individual human being, the Kingdom of God is to human society. That kingdom represents what society can potentially become just as the image of God represents what the individual can become. When there is transformation of individuals on a massive scale through the release of human potential — when the latent capacities for loving and knowing are organised and expressed on a social level as the progressive eradication of prejudice — we advance towards the establishment of the Kingdom of God on earth.

Bahá'u'lláh's Revelation did not deal only with the transformation of the individual in a vacuum; this would be extremely difficult, if not impossible. He also provided a blueprint for building a new world order. That building process is directed and guided by Bahá'í institutions in a way that will enable society to become its true self — the Kingdom of God on earth. The response to anxieties and tests on an individual basis also has a social counterpart. Social institutions have their tests too; and their development depends on whether or not they can take that creative step into the unknown and form new kinds of legislation sustained by new kinds of judicial supports.

*As greater and greater numbers of human beings find a way through the Bahá'í Faith to become their own true selves, society will also be in the process of becoming its true self: the Kingdom of God on earth.*

Bahá'ís accept the Kingdom of God on earth as a reality ultimately attainable, not through a passive waiting for it to happen to us in an instant by some miracle, but through dedicated efforts over a long period of time to become what we can become in the face of many trials and tribulations. Those who make these dedicated efforts feel themselves able to play an active part in the greatest miracle of all — conscious acceptance of the responsibility to become knowing and loving servants of humanity for the glorification of God.

Thus, as greater and greater numbers of human beings find a way through the Bahá'í Faith to become their own true selves — to reflect the image of God in their lives — society will also be in the process of becoming its true self: the Kingdom of God on earth.

*If the travellers seek after the goal of the Intended One...this station appertaineth to the self — but that self which is 'The Self of God standing within Him with laws'.*

*On this plane, the self is not rejected but beloved; it is well-pleasing and not to be shunned. Although at the beginning, this plane is the realm of conflict, yet it endeth in attainment to the throne of splendour...*

*This is the plane of the self which is well-pleasing unto God. Refer to the verse:*

*'Oh, thou soul which art at rest,*
*Return to thy Lord, well-pleased, and pleasing Him . . .*
*Enter thou among My servants,*
*And enter thou My paradise.'*[9]

Bahá'u'lláh

O My servants! Could ye apprehend with what wonders of My munificence and bounty I have willed to entrust your souls, ye would, of a truth, rid yourselves of attachment to all created things, and would gain a true knowledge of your own selves — a knowledge which is the same as the comprehension of Mine own Being. Ye would find yourselves independent of all else but Me, and would perceive, with your inner and outer eye, and as manifest as the revelation of My effulgent Name, the sea of My loving-kindness and bounty moving within you.[10]

Bahá'u'lláh

# REFERENCES

1. David R. Barrett, 'World Religious Statistics', *1988 Britannica Book of the Year*, p. 303. This lists the Bahá'í Faith as having 'significant communities' in 205 countries, compared to 254 for Christianity and 172 for Islám. Since publication of these figures, Bahá'í communities have been established and officially recognised in the countries of Central and Eastern Europe, and in those of the former Soviet Union, further raising this number. Statisticians at the Bahá'í World Centre calculated in 1992 that the Bahá'í Faith is now established in 232 countries and dependent territories.

2. Bahá'u'lláh, *The Hidden Words*, trans. Shoghi Effendi 'with the assistance of some English friends' (London: Nightingale Books, 1992) p. 3.

3. Bahá'u'lláh, *The Seven Valleys*, trans. Marzieh Gail in consultation with Ali Kuli Khan (London: Nightingale Books, 1992) p. 89.

4. Bahá'u'lláh, *The Hidden Words*, p. 30.

5. Ibid., p. 3.

6. Bahá'u'lláh, *The Kitáb-i-Aqdas; The Most Holy Book*, trans. Shoghi Effendi et al., (London: Bahá'í Publishing Trust, rev. ed., 1993) p. 85.

7. Bahá'u'lláh, *The Hidden Words*, p. 20.

8. Ibid.

9. Bahá'u'lláh, 'The Four Valleys', from *The Seven Valleys and the Four Valleys*, trans. Marzieh Gail in consultation with Ali Kuli Khan, (Wilmette, Ill: Bahá'í Publishing Trust, 3rd rev. ed., 1978) p. 50. The verse quoted is from the Qur'án 89: 27-30.

10. Bahá'u'lláh, *Gleanings from the Writings of Bahá'u'lláh*, comp. and trans. Shoghi Effendi (Wilmette, Ill: Bahá'í Publishing Trust, 2nd ed., 1976) pp. 326-7.

# FURTHER READING

## THE BAHÁ'ÍS
*Bahá'í International Community, Office of Public Information*
This magazine-format publication offers a rich variety of photographs, charts and diagrams illustrating the origin, development, current state and future prospects of the Bahá'í community around the globe, as well as presenting an overview of its main beliefs, practices and goals.
*Bahá'í Publishing Trust, UK*
*80pp; 28 x 21cm; sc; 1-870989-37-6; £2.50*

## THE PROMISE OF WORLD PEACE
*The Universal House of Justice*
This succinct inquiry into the condition of the world today shows how 'an urge towards unity, like a spiritual springtime, struggles to express itself', compelling nations, peoples and races to overcome traditional barriers of hostility and work together for the common good.
*Bahá'í Publishing Trust, USA*
*40pp; 23 x 18cm; sc; 0-900125-68-3; £3.50*

## THE HIDDEN WORDS
*Bahá'u'lláh, with paintings by Jacqueline Craske*
A treasury of epigrams in which Bahá'u'lláh simply and clearly communicates the essence of spiritual wisdom throughout the ages. The central ethical text of the Bahá'í Faith, a daily source of guidance for millions around the world.
*Nightingale Books*
*112pp; 16 x 13cm; sc; 0-900125-93-4; £5.95*

## THE SEVEN VALLEYS
*Bahá'u'lláh, with paintings by Rob Hain*
This delightful and uplifting book guides the seeker through the valleys of Search, Love, Knowledge, Unity, Contentment, and Wonderment, to the goal of reunion with our Creator in the valley of True Poverty and Absolute Nothingness.
*Nightingale Books*
*128pp; 17 x 11cm; sc; 1-870989-16-3; £5.95*

These books can be obtained from Bahá'ís in your area, or from bookshops and libraries. Alternatively, you may order them direct from: The Bahá'í Publishing Trust, 6 Mount Pleasant, Oakham, Leicestershire LE15 6HU, United Kingdom. Free catalogue available on request.